Canada from Above

A Photo Journey

Heather Patterson

Scholastic Canada Ltd.
Toronto New York London Auckland Sydney
Mexico City New Delhi Hong Kong Buenos Aires

For Lily — who notices every little thing
— H.P.

Photo Credits

Cover: Rolf Hicker Photography
Page 1: Courtesy of NASA/GSFC/LaRC/JPL, MISR Team
Page 2: Rolf Hicker/All Canada Photos
Pages 3, 5 and 12: Ron Garnett – AirScapes
Pages 4, 7, 8, 14 and 18: Jim Wark – AirphotoNA
Pages 6 and 21: Barrett & MacKay/All Canada Photos
Page 9: Roy Tanami/Ursus Photography
Page 10: Chris Cheadle/All Canada Photos
Page 11: Norbert Rosing/National Geographic Stock
Pages 13, 16, 22, 23 and 26: Russ Heinl/All Canada Photos
Page 15: Courtesy of John Steadman
Page 17: David Boyer/National Geographic Stock
Pages 19 and 24: Courtesy of Diavik Diamond Mines Inc.
Page 20: Courtesy of Natalie Haney – Alberta Pond Hockey
Association
Page 25: Medford Taylor/National Geographic Stock
Page 27: Robert Postma/First Light
Page 28: Ian McAllister/All Canada Photos
Page 29 and back cover: Paul Hoffman/Lone Pine Photo
Page 30: Michael Poliza/National Geographic Stock

Library and Archives Canada Cataloguing in Publication

Patterson, Heather, 1945-
      Canada from above : a photo journey / Heather Patterson.
ISBN 978-1-4431-0224-7
      1. Canada--Aerial photographs--Juvenile literature.
2. Canada--Pictorial works--Juvenile literature. I. Title.
FC59.P37 2010   j917.10022'2   C2010-901643-2

6 5 4 3 2 1   Printed in Canada 119   10 11 12 13 14

FSC — Mixed Sources
Product group from well-managed
forests, controlled sources and
recycled wood or fiber
www.fsc.org Cert no. SGS-COC-003098
© 1996 Forest Stewardship Council

A view from above — from a satellite, airplane or helicopter — is an overview in more ways than one. An overview can mean an explanation that sums up the whole of an object or an idea. And that is what an aerial view does so well: it explains at a glance something we could not have understood at eye level.

In this book, you are invited to fly over Canada for a look at some fascinating features of our vast and varied country — from above. On every page, you can look down on something either natural or man-made, and understand it better. And on every page, you will see beauty, order and design. Enjoy the overview!

A satellite looks down on a unique feature of Canada — the Manicouagan impact crater, believed to have been caused by an asteroid 212 million years ago. It formed Lake Manicouagan, a ring of water circling a huge island, sometimes called the "eye of Quebec."

Looking directly down at a small island near Thunder Bay, Ontario, and through the clear waters of Lake Superior that surround it, we are reminded that islands don't float; they are firmly attached to Earth's base.

At low tide, the tidal flats at Lower Wedgeport, Nova Scotia, look empty of life. But millions of organisms thrive just below the mud's surface, providing a feast for shorebirds. At high tide, the flats are covered with sea water, full of nutrients and marine life.

In 1731 the Hudson's Bay Company began building Prince of Wales Fort to guard their cargo ships at the mouth of the Churchill River, where it empties into Hudson Bay in northern Manitoba. It ended up taking more than 40 years. Though the fort was partially destroyed in 1782, it has since been restored.

At Quebec City's highest point, the Citadelle sits like a star overlooking the St. Lawrence River. Behind it lie the Plains of Abraham. The fortification was built between 1820 and 1831 by the British, to defend the strategic heights from the Americans. Today it is still occupied by troops.

Modern machinery handles the job of harrowing potatoes near Nine Mile Creek, Prince Edward Island, moving down the length of a field in precise lines. Humans have been growing and harvesting plants for food for at least 10,000 years.

In recent years, humans have begun to farm fish. Circular cages in the ocean off the coast of New Brunswick contain thousands of salmon — swimming, feeding and growing until they are ready for market. Wild Atlantic salmon have become endangered, so salmon farming helps to supply the demand around the world.

Bordered by autumn trees, granite is removed from the Earth at a stone quarry in southern Quebec, in a pattern of precise, square-cornered cuts. The stone, more than 350 million years old, will be used for homes, office buildings and other structures.

On an August day in Nunavut, the waters of the Hood River tumble down Wilberforce Falls on their way to the Arctic Ocean. The great gorge was created by natural forces more than 500 million years ago. A carpet of tundra plants, reddened by frost, spreads on either side.

In massive rafts called log booms, huge timbers harvested from British Columbia's forests are arrayed side by side and end to end to make their way down the Fraser River to Vancouver.

Every summer, as soon as the pack ice has melted away, as many as 2000 belugas gather in the shallow waters at the mouth of the Cunningham River on Somerset Island in Nunuvut. Here they stay for about a month, playing, nursing their young and rolling on the gravel bottom to moult their skin.

More than 100 years ago, Europeans immigrated to the Canadian prairies to build homes and farm the land. Today, in Fairy Glen, Saskatchewan, their descendants weather the winter in a farmhouse amid an organized cluster of barns, storage sheds and steel grain bins.

More than 1000 years ago, Vikings crossed the Atlantic and became the first Europeans to build a settlement in North America. It was at L'Anse aux Meadows, at the tip of Newfoundland's Great Northern Peninsula. Today it is a World Heritage Site featuring reconstructions of the Vikings' sod houses, workshops and a small forge.

Descending from its headwaters in the Rocky Mountains, the Fraser River twists and turns its way through the Robson Valley in east-central British Columbia, between the Cariboo Mountains and the Rockies.

Four giant waterslides twist and turn their way down to splashy endings. They were designed for Ontario Place — an entertainment complex built on three man-made islands at the edge of Toronto in Lake Ontario.

15

Bridges cross the North Saskatchewan River into Edmonton, the capital of Alberta. More than 80 per cent of Canadians live in cities; more than one million of them live in Edmonton's metropolitan area.

The hamlet of Aklavik, "the place of the barren-ground grizzly bears" in the Northwest Territories, can only be reached by plane or by a winter ice road from Inuvik, across the frozen streams of the Mackenzie Delta. It began as a Hudson's Bay Company trading post in 1912. Today it is home to about 600 people, mainly Inuvialuit and Gwich'in Dene.

The *Maid of the Mist* offers a close-up view of Horseshoe Falls to sightseers at Niagara Falls, Ontario. Every second, millions of litres of water flow toward the giant curve of rock and take a thundering 50-metre plunge to continue along the Niagara River to Lake Ontario.

The Diavik Diamond Mine sits on an island surrounded by the shallow waters of Lac de Gras. To mine the kimberlite ore which contains the diamonds, dikes were built first, to hold back the water around the open pits. Summer in the subarctic Northwest Territories is short; for most of the year, ice and snow grip the region.

Every February, the Alberta Pond Hockey Tournament celebrates the game of hockey on frozen Lac Cardinal, in the Peace Region of northern Alberta. In 2010, 78 teams competed on 20 rinks for a chance to play in the World Pond Hockey Championships in Plaster Rock, New Brunswick.

While summer visitors enjoy the fine beaches at Cape Traverse, Prince Edward Island, others must work: beyond the rippled sands of the ocean's edge, farmers plant their crops in neat fields, and fishermen harvest the crops of the sea.

The Parliament Buildings sit grandly on top of Parliament Hill, overlooking the Ottawa River. Construction began in 1860, three years after Queen Victoria chose Ottawa to be the capital of Canada. The current Parliament Buildings were completed in 1927, after a fire in 1916 destroyed all but the circular library.

A cluster of boats, wharves and stages proclaims the fishing heritage of Burgeo, a town of 1600 on the south coast of Newfoundland. For thousands of years indigenous peoples lived and fished on the island. About 500 years ago, Burgeo was discovered by Portuguese fishing ships, and in the 1790s Europeans settled here to make a living from the sea.

Every January in the Northwest Territories, a 600-kilometre-long ice road is built from Yellowknife north to the diamond mines. Beginning in February, and for only eight to ten weeks, an entire year of supplies and equipment must be trucked up this road. In the spring, the ice road begins to melt into the lakes, ponds and spongy tundra that it was built over, and by summer it has disappeared.

Near Thunder Bay, Ontario, an icebreaker carves a path through the ice that covers parts of Lake Superior each winter. Canada has 21 icebreakers, designed and built for specific Canadian needs. Because Thunder Bay is a major port in the Great Lakes St. Lawrence Seaway System, icebreakers are used here to keep shipping channels open.

In the badlands
near Drumheller in
southeastern Alberta,
the walls of Horsethief
Canyon rise to fields of
wheat and canola that
stretch to the horizon.
The canyon's ancient
layers of sedimentary rock
were exposed by glacial
erosion 12,000 years ago.
Wind, water, freezing
and thawing, plus the
semi-arid climate,
continue to reveal the
bones of dinosaurs.

In northwest Saskatchewan, the William River reveals a stunning floor of sculpted sand beneath its clear waters. It runs through a northern desert in Athabasca Sand Dunes Provincial Wilderness Park, where mammoth dune fields rise as high as 30 metres, shifting constantly with the wind, and encroaching on forests of spruce and pine.

Western red cedars, Sitka spruce and coast Douglas-firs can tower as tall as 100 metres. These old-growth giants of the Great Bear Rainforest on British Columbia's coast provide shelter for grizzlies, black bears and Kermode bears, a rare white-coated variation of the black bear.

The Kaskawulsh glacier in Kluane National Park, Yukon, is a massive river of ice, flowing so slowly through the St. Elias Mountains that movement is undetectable. Like all glaciers, it was formed over many centuries by layers of densely packed snow. Where the two arms converge, it is five to six kilometres wide.

This is not a flock of strange birds flying over a forest. You are looking at belugas swimming over aquatic vegetation in Hudson Bay near Churchill, Manitoba.

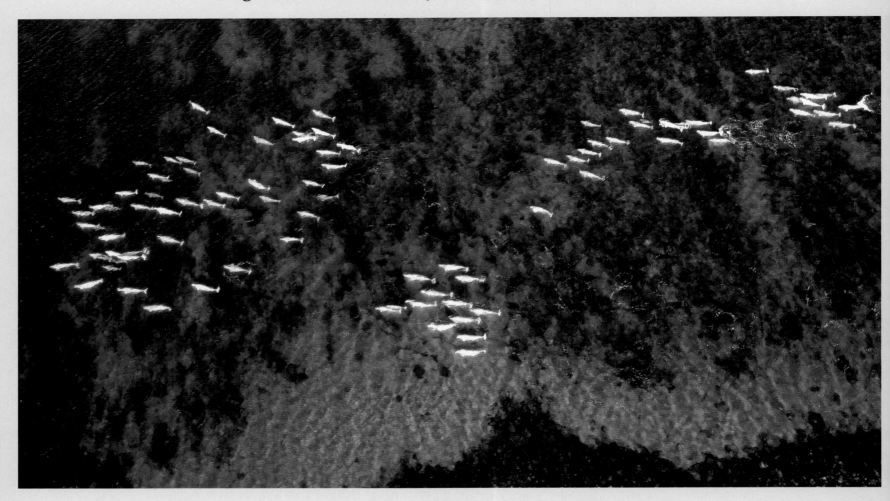

An overview can surprise, inform, or even fool you. It's always worth a second look!